MIXED FEELINGS

An Illustrated Guide for
Biracial and Multiracial Kids and Their Families

Written and Illustrated by
Teja Arboleda, MEd

For more information on the author and his company, Entertaining Diversity, Inc., please visit: www.EntertainingDiversity.com

Written and Illustrated by Teja Arboleda, MEd
Edited by Barbara Wilson Arboleda, MS CCC-SLP
Copyedited by Marlis Jörgensen Arboleda

Entertaining Diversity Press is a subsidiary of Entertaining Diversity, Inc.

ISBN-13: 978-0692755044
ISBN-10: 0692755047

Dedicated to:

All of the mixed kids and mixed families who prove everyday that love and life transcend all the limitations of racial categories.

Special Thanks:

My wife Barbara with whom I've built an amazing mixed family in a foreign world.

My daughter Katie who gives me a universe of opportunities to be the best Daddy on the planet.

My mother Marlis who provided me with guidance and love in a segregated world.

My father Amadio who showed me how to face discrimination and intolerance with strength and conviction.

My brother Miguel who was the best kuya/sempai/big brother a boy could have.

The countless audience members, students and readers who support my work.

The Census Bureau - for giving me the courage to *not* choose a race.

Kids: For You, Like No Other

Hey kids! Being mixed is awesome. Of course it is, because you're unique and belong to many at the same time! You can look in the mirror and say, "Yes, I'm many!" You are a hero because you bring people from all over the world together!

But sometimes you may find that your friends and others don't understand what race or **culture** you are. And that can feel confusing. Even those who love you and teach you may not know what it's like being mixed, and may not know how to talk about being **biracial**, **multiracial** or **cross-racially adopted**.

Mixed Feelings is about a group of kids who are a lot like you in some ways. They can help you learn how to share and express some of your feelings and ideas about being mixed! Their lives take place in school, on the playground, at home with their families, and most of all, with each other. You may recognize some of your life experiences in their stories, and through them you can learn some new ways to help people understand you better. After all, being mixed can be a happy, healthy part of who you are.

Let's Dive Into The Mix!

PARENTS: GUARDIANS & EDUCATORS

Mixed Feelings is an illustrated book for **mixed-race** and **mixed-culture** children, their parents and guardians, told through heart-warming and realistic stories and scenarios. *Mixed Feelings* is an entertaining guide that offers a new perspective on the ways in which mixed children may be misunderstood, and offers suggestions for the ways in which these children, their families and classmates can best thrive in their communities.

In addition to positive and exciting experiences, mixed kids can often have ambiguous, sometimes even negative thoughts about being mixed. Mixed kids might be questioned, encouraged, even bullied into making a decision as to *what* they are, to the exclusion of other parts of their identity. It is not necessarily helpful to only praise the multi-identity that kids may have. Rather, they need help dealing with the confusion they or others may experience in the future.

To illustrate some of the challenges and delights of mixed-race kids, this book focuses on a group of fictionalized characters, at school, in their neighborhoods and in their homes. Their stories deal with a diversity of family patterns, including **mixed-race**, **mixed-culture** and **cross-racial adoption** through social interactions, school issues, friendships, **cultural biases**, secrets and discovery. The chapters are organized in modules, to help young readers and their families face curiosity about them as *other*, deal with stress of being bullied for that reason, recognize the positives and **assets** of being mixed and build **empathy** and **resilience**.

*All words and phrases in **bold** and red appear in the Key Words section.*

HELLO!

Hi kids! I'm Chamix, and I'm here to show you around. Yes, I am a **chameleon**!

Welcome to Fairview, my town. It has a lot of kids just like you who will show you how they deal with being mixed. Their parents might look different from each other. Their grandparents might have come from different parts of the world. They might even be adopted or speak two or more languages at home and practice different religions. Or even all of the above! I know a lot of people here, and I'm so happy to be your personal tour guide.

JUMP INTO THE MIX!

SAM

Hi everybody, my name is Samantha, but I prefer Sam. I'm kinda shy... Well, my sister and I were born in Boston. My Papa is a carpenter, and he lets me help him when he is working on a house nearby. I hand him tools when he is on the ladder. When he's home he tells us stories. Nana is Papa's Ma, and she loves talking about her country, Ireland. My other Grandma and Grandpa live in The Philippines. That's where Mama is from. Mama works long days as a nurse. There is always someone sick who needs her help at the hospital. My sister Lily is older than I am, but she is the best, except when she tells me what to do. Oh, and I'm nine years old.

Sam feels that the places that hold her heart are The Philippines, Ireland and Boston. Her family just moved to this new town and she and they don't know anybody else yet. Which places hold your heart?

LILY

Hi guys! Did Sam tell you our last name is Kelly? I'm eleven. Papa is Irish and Mama is Filipino and Chinese. We just moved from Boston. I like to make new friends. I have friends in Boston of course and in The Philippines too because we visit Grandma and Grandpa. Soon I'll have friends here too.

Lily, who has the same parents as Sam, thinks of herself as Eurasian. Nana, Dad's Mom, speaks Irish and English. Lily and Sam also understand some words in Tagalog, the language of their Filipino/Chinese grandparents. Do you speak or know some words in different languages?

GRACE

Hiya! I am Grace Grayson and I'm ten and I'm from Fairview. My parents adopted me from China when I was just a baby. They are the only parents I know. I don't know why sometimes people ask me to say something in Chinese. China is way on the other side of the planet! How can I say something in Chinese when I've been speaking only English my whole life? My Mom works at the town newspaper and Dad is an engineer. Mom says I can be anything I want when I grow up. My secret dream is to be an actress, but I could be a teacher too or maybe a scientist. Sometimes people who don't know us can't tell we're a family because I don't look like my parents. But my parents really love me and tell me everyday. Sometimes it's embarrassing...They don't have to keep telling me. But I guess it makes them feel good and me too.

Grace lives with her Mom and Dad, but she quietly wishes she had a brother or sister. She knows she is from China, and looks Chinese, but she's proud of being American. She is learning baton twirling and will be in the 4th of July parade this year, celebrating our independence from England. Is there anybody adopted in your family?

ETHAN

I'm Ethan, hey, what's happnin'? I live with my Mom, and we visit Grandma sometimes. That's it, that's my family. Mom says she's looking for a new father for me. That's okay with me if she wants to, but I don't really care. People ask me about my father but he is not around. I think he's Black. Anyway, I wish they wouldn't ask that question. Oh yeah, I'm ten. If you need to know more you can ask my Mom. She's part Polish and Russian and she's Jewish. My Grandma likes to teach me words in Yiddish.

Ethan sees himself as a team with his Mom. Okay, his grandmother is on the team too. Ethan's Dad is African-American. His Dad and Mom broke up when he was just a baby. He doesn't remember much about him. His Dad lives in another state and has remarried. Is there anyone in your family who has remarried or separated?

LUIS

My turn. I'm Luis Washington. I'm twelve and I've got this great family. Mi Madre es Cubana. From her side of the family, we have all this great food, music, lots of cousins, lots of laughing and fun. My Dad's Black. He tells me I am supposed to tell you I'm African-American but I kind of like being both. He's cool though. He taught me how to play basketball and we hang out whenever we can. My sister and brother are both in high school. Her name is Catalina, but everybody calls her Cat for short. She is a junior and very popular. Mi hermano, Danny, is a freshman. Danny is an honor student, and won't let you forget it. And Cat's the creative one. I'm the one who likes to make people happy. In our family it's never boring - I like it that way.

Luis feels like a citizen of the world. He comes from two cultures and embraces them both. Even though he speaks Spanish fluently, he sometimes avoids it because some kids make fun of him about it. Lucky for him, he can **code-switch** easily between languages almost without thinking. Some people code-switch languages like Luis. Other people code-switch by changing some of their behaviors depending on who they are with. In what ways do you code-switch at home or with your friends?

OLIVER

OK, OK, I'm last! What else is new! I'm just kidding. My name is Oliver Shuman. I'm ten. Our family is small but also larger than most. My little sister Kaia is three years old. There's Ma, Dad and my dog, Peanut, and of course me. That's my immediate family. Dad's side of the family is really large. Peanut is a Labradoodle and she goes everywhere with me, except school. They don't let me bring her there. I wish they would, because Peanut gets lonely without me. My Dad is a Native American from the Hopi Tribe, and my Mom is German-American.

Oliver has a Mom and Dad, and a sister, and of course his dog Peanut. He sometimes thinks of Sarah, his friend and neighbor, as another sister. Oliver has lots of cousins but they don't live close by. Do you have a pet that you love like a family member?

CHAPTER 1: RACE IS ON!

Before we get into the stories about our new friends, let's review a few things. We first have to learn how *we* describe *ourselves*, and then you can teach me how how *you* describe *you*! But first...*me*!

As a chameleon, **adapting** to the environment is my kind of thing. You might not know that one way in which we chameleons communicate is by changing color. Can you imagine what it's like when I'm with all my friends? When I'm on the disco floor with all the lights changing, and the mirror ball...it's exhausting! I think you'd find it exhausting too, if you had to constantly adapt to everything...and everyone around you...!

We just moved from Japan. Some kids in the new school asked me questions about what race I am. I've never been asked that before. My Dad is Japanese and my Mom is White American. What should I say?
Kenji in Baltimore, Maryland

Boxes

So what are these labels? Why do we have them? Well, a long time ago, way after dinosaurs but way before Facebook and Instagram, some scientists believed that human beings could be divided into different **races** - **Caucasian**, **Asian** and **Black**. (Actually, a long, long time ago, it was Caucasoid, Mongolische and Negroid.) Eventually more races were added. The list is now quite large, but the ones most people consider are: Asian, Black, **Hispanic**, **Native American** and **White**. They defined these races based on things like skin color, hair texture, eye shape, and nose shape. In other words, how you physically appear to others. That might make it complicated for some people, especially if they're mixed. Then not that long ago the label **Other** was created for people who are more than one - a mix - also called biracial and multiracial.

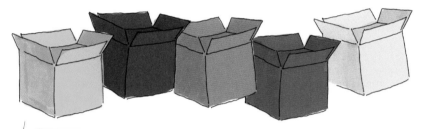

Speaking of colors, I'm looking at some boxes here. Which one is Other? If an alien landed on planet earth and saw you, I don't think the alien would say, "Hello Other!"

Other

The term Other might make you feel like you don't belong. What you look like shouldn't make you feel different. Not all people of one race look the same. There are millions of different shades of skin color. And sometimes, a person who is White may actually be darker than someone who is Black. And many people might get darker in the summer and their hair might change color with exposure to the sun. Often mixed-race people are thought to be a race that they are not.

DIVERSITY

Why is the word **diversity** important to know? Because diversity is everywhere. No two galaxies are alike. No two stars are alike. No two planets, clouds, mountains, trees, cows, cats, ferrets, snowflakes or burritos are alike. No two people are alike, even identical twins! So being mixed is actually the most common thing in the world. Diversity means understanding and accepting that each individual is unique, and recognizing our individual differences.

WORDS

Biracial
(**bi** meaning two)
If your parents are each of a different race.

Multiracial
(**multi** meaning two or more)
If one or both of your parents are of two or more races.

Cross-racial adoption
If you were adopted and you are a different race than your parents.

WAKE-UP CALL

It's early in the morning, and you're getting ready for school. You're barely awake. You have a quick bite of yesterday's peanut butter sandwich. You look in the mirror to comb your hair, and realize there's peanut butter stuck to your nose. And then you realize that your nose is a lot like your father's... without the peanut butter. It's the same shape. But then you look at your beautiful eyes and you realize that your eyes are like your mother's. And your mouth is like hers, but your hair is like your father's. And your skin...it's somewhere in between. And now you're late for school. Now, I eat flies and other insects, so peanut butter is not my problem. Just stop putting peanut butter on (or in) your nose!

> Why do people always say President Obama is Black? Isn't he White and Black?
>
> Simone in Lincoln, Nebraska

HERO

What you may not have thought about, however, is race. If your father is Black and your mother is Asian, it's not really on your mind. But other people seeing you all together might see that you are different races. So some people notice, and some don't. Mixed people often look **ambiguous**. Oliver is aware that most people don't know he's part Native American. He's very shy, and he doesn't like to talk about it.

US President Barack Obama is biracial and multicultural. He was raised by his mother and grandmother who were both White. His father was Black, but not American because he was actually from Kenya, in Africa. And the President grew up partly in Indonesia, which is in Southeast Asia, with his mother and stepfather.

Being mixed is a powerful thing. Look at you, you superhero! Bringing people together like nobody's business! Race is mostly about facial features, your appearance and how people see each of you. When you're feeling really confused about how you fit in with other groups, just remember that you have a lot in common with more people than you can imagine!

BRAIN PICKINGS

- Have you ever wondered about your racial mix?
- What do you know about your racial mix?
- What race do people think you are when they first meet you?
- What kinds of things do people say or what questions do they ask you about your race?
- Has anyone ever asked you ridiculous questions like, "Which parts of you are Black and White"?

My Mom taught me this: Close your eyes for 30 seconds. Remind yourself how awesome your mix is. Now imagine all the generations of people before you all over the world who made you what you are. You'll never feel alone!
Anandi in Austin, Texas

Chapter 2: Culture Splash

You might speak two or more languages, listen to quiet elevator music and eat salty fish heads, tofu and seaweed...mmmm...dragonflies...I like eating insects...Ooops! Sorry. I got distracted. You might bow when you say hello to your family, and take your shoes off in the house. These things you practice are part of your culture. But culture is not determined by what you look like. In America we have all kinds of people who may look very different from each other, and who may be of the same culture as you.

Want vs Must

There is **want-to-do culture** and **must-do culture**.

A **want-to-do culture** example is, "I want to eat a five-cheese-pizza with my family and watch a movie like we do every Thursday." A more common want-to-do culture might be something like having sleepovers and Halloween trick-or-treating. Some cultures don't practice these things.

A **must-do culture** example is, "I must clean up after dinner because that is one of my household chores." And a more common must-do culture would be something like saying 'hello' or even bowing low to someone when you're introduced to them.

But wait! I forgot about **don't-wanna-do culture**. An example of that is, "I don't want to floss and brush my teeth because I'm lazy and I don't care about having teeth, even if I have to sip my crispy French fries through a straw."

In our apartment we keep our shoes on...except when I'm in bed or taking a shower, of course. But my neighbor Mikiko who moved here from Japan, takes her shoes off in her apartment, and even my place, when she comes over. But some kids think that just because we're both Asian, that I should take my shoes off in our apartment.
Ji-Min in New York, NY

Mini Cultures

Do you have a secret handshake? I know you do! That's like a mini culture. You and your friends have a private, fun thing to do, and it makes you a group with a **group culture**. Just remember that the group and culture can change many times, over time. You probably won't be doing that same handshake when you're 50 years old!

Adapting

You know, as a chameleon, I can change how I look, and blend in almost instantly. What I can't do is change who I am. Like you, I'm just... me. I will always enjoy hanging upside down on a twig, waiting for the perfect buzzing, squiggling meal to fly within my tongue's range. And talking to you of course!

Cultures are things you and your family or best friends, or even community, practice and celebrate. For example, if your father is Jewish and your mother is Christian, that would be a mixed-cultural setting. Some people might not know how you practice all those things between both faiths, but they eventually will, even if it gets complicated sometimes. That's when **compromise** kicks in. In all situations where people of different backgrounds get together, everyone has to compromise a little, bend a little, adapt and adopt a little, understand and **empathize** a little. When we act upon these important things in a selfless manner, it makes us good and understanding human beings. That's how we learn to live with each other - as different friends and different families, different communities and different countries.

MIX + MIX = MIX

So here's what's going to bake your tofu: You can be multiracial AND multicultural! If anything, that makes you especially unique because you can code-switch and maybe even speak different languages and make all kinds of friends. For example, there are many Black Jews living in the United States. Many people think a person's race can determine a person's religion. That's not true at all!

Sometimes I get all knotted up when I have to explain why I lived in different places. I just want to make friends and stay in one place.
Angela in Hartford, CT

You might also be a **TCK**, which stands for **Third Culture Kid**, which means that you had been or are now growing up in different countries/cultures that might be different from your parents'. TCKs often speak more than one language and feel comfortable when traveling to different countries. Wow, I could really enjoy riding a double-decker bus in London, England right now! Or maybe eating sushi in downtown Kyoto, Japan!

Sometimes people don't understand how you can be so many things, when in fact, you are just...*you*. A singular human being with a lot of really cool things that make you connected to many peoples, cultures, places, but unique at the same time. So instead of being an octopus that has many arms, you have many cultures and identities that all work in concert!

WHAT'S YOUR MIX?

YOU = YOU

It's most important to remember that you are *you*. You don't have to be anybody else. As you go through your pre-teen and teen years, there will be many, many (...did I say *many*?) moments that you will be unsure about *what* and *who* you are. Everyone goes through that. As long as you do the things that make you happy, that are safe, make you feel good, then you as a many-cultures-person will be okay. Just don't let other people tell you what culture you're supposed to be or practice. *You be you!*

BRAIN PICKINGS

- What culture or cultures do people usually think you are?
- What are some "don't-wanna-do cultures" that describe you?
- Do you have any want-to-do cultures? What are they?
- Does your family practice any must-do cultures at home or with other people? What are they?
- If you've lived in different cultures or countries, do you feel that being mixed makes it easier to blend in? Why or why not?

20

Chapter 3: What Me Is Me?

Hello Me!

$$x \frac{(me + what)}{we - most} \sqrt{omg}$$

Since the dawn of time, humans of all cultures and ages have asked that important question: "Who am I?" Mixed people have the option of also asking the question, "What am I?" The answer of course, is simple - human. I of course say chameleon, unless I'm really hungry, which I always am, and then I call myself tiger. Very often, we feel we have to identify our race and culture. While not necessary, it can be empowering and fun to explore. When you round the corner of becoming a teenager, more and more you might be compelled to ask these two questions that even Shakespeare asked, in many ways (do your best Shakespeare delivery): "Who is't am I? For what am I?"

Inside Scoop

There are so many ways in which we learn about our races and cultures. Through family first, then friends and the community. You might have conversations about grandparents, cousins, about where they grew up and some of the awesome and also sometimes difficult things they might have had to deal with. Television, movies and videos are big influences on you too. You of course already know that most television and movies are not real - actors portray the characters and very often those actors look only one particular way. In fact, you can probably identify the type of character an actor portrays within the first minute of a new TV series.

Mixed people don't see a lot of actors who look like them because mixed people are racially ambiguous. Television and the movies often focus on characters that are very clearly one thing - one race or culture. Those are **archetypical** characters. Then there are **stereotypical** characters - the characters who are made fun of because of their archetypical character. For example, the nerdy Asian girl with thick glasses, who's good at math; the Black boy who's great at dancing; or the blond girl who's not very smart. After-school television shows are particularly meant to be funny, with a laugh track, and often rely on archetypes and stereotypes. Many movies, like Disney's *Pocahontas* are filled with stereotypes and are not factual. Our friend Oliver, as part Native American, is very concerned about this particular matter.

A more complicated issue is that mixed-race child actors may be told they have to *act* like someone that they're not - to fit into a role that others might think represents *what* they are or what they're supposed to be. For example, a kid that is Japanese-American and White American may be directed to act more "Asian" or speak with an accent. Or worse, if there's a mixed Asian and Black boy, the producers might make him a nerdy Asian who also dances really well. These scenes would certainly be confusing for the actor, but you the viewer as well.

CODE BREAKER

There's a lot of pressure for young people to choose sides, wear certain clothes, act a certain way, speak in code. Forming groups can be fun, but keeping the group together can sometimes be tricky. Imagine if the groups were formed based on what you look like. Mixed kids can be sometimes left out in these ways.

The stereotypes of any particular group can seem overwhelming. For mixed kids, those sides might have to do with race - how people see you. Being true to yourself means also being proud of all the things you are. You can help your friends or group, or even the whole school understand that you don't have to be just one thing. Guaranteed, there will be many kids just like you who will really appreciate it!

Personal Math

Oliver and his Mom sat in the dining room working on fractions for his homework. After finishing his practice problems, he put down his pencil and asked, "Remember a while ago Dad said he was three-fourths Hopi and a quarter White? What does that make me?"

"Add to that, I'm Swedish and German," said his Mom, sipping coffee.

Oliver thought for a moment and pulled out a piece of paper. "So, if half of me is three-quarters Hopi, then… ." He scribbled some figures on the page. "I'm three-eighths Hopi. Is that enough?"

His Mom put down her mug. "Enough for what, sweetheart?"

"Enough to say I'm Hopi. Maybe I'm not Hopi enough."

"Well, your Dad is on the Hopi Membership Roll. And you need to be at least one quarter Hopi to be able to become a member yourself. So, what do you think?"

Oliver looked at his numbers. "Well, two-eighths would equal one quarter. So, I'm more than one quarter Hopi." He looked down at the table. "Does everyone have to keep track of these percentages and things?"

His Mom smiled. "More important is how you feel about your heritage and how connected you feel to Hopi culture."

"I don't know how I feel about it."

"You don't have to yet. You'll figure it out in time. Numbers aside, it's about your mind and heart."

"I guess," Oliver said and he started packing up his books and papers for school the next day. "Can I go fishing with Dad on Saturday?"

"Of course, young man. You can have a bonding day - ask him more about it then. I'm sure he'd love to share stories with you."

This And That

Sometimes mixed people feel they need to figure out mathematically what percentage they are this or that, and then they might feel like they need to be very loyal to those parts of their culture. **So instead of this OR that, think about yourself as this AND that.** It's difficult enough to understand everything about one culture, and certainly more difficult to understand all the cultures and races you are. Just making new friends and enjoying time with them helps you connect on levels that are just human!

Brain Pickings

- How do you know what the different parts are of your racial and cultural makeup?
- Have you ever seen a mixed person who was represented kindly on television or in the movies?
- Do you have a special code language between you and some friends? Is it different from codes with other friends?
- If you knew more about your different cultures or races, do you think you'd be a different person?
- What kinds of archetypical characters are common on TV and the movies?
- What stereotypes make you cringe and maybe even feel bad?

Chapter 4: Me Many

It can be tricky feeling like you suddenly belong to a group. For one thing, you might not be sure how you all fit together. Sam and Lily just moved to town, and they don't really know many other kids. And Grace has her own particular story that sometimes pops up - questions she has to answer often, even though it shouldn't be that way.

A lot of the girls in my school dress like some of those characters on TV who dont look like me. I tried to wear those clothes, but they said it doesnt fit who I am. How do they think I should be dressing?
Noriko in Chapel Hill, North Carolina

COOL MIX

One of the cool things about being mixed is that you can find similarities between you and all kinds of people. As a kid you're already making up stories in your head or with your friends - adventures, characters, celebrities, inventors. Friends who like to be with you because of who you are, are the best friends you can have.

Let's take a look at how Lily, Sam and Grace become friends, regardless of their racial and cultural differences.

COUNT ME IN!

Sam was lying under her covers, moping. Lily heard Sam sigh loudly and came into her room and sat on her bed by her feet.

"What's wrong?" Lily asked.

Sam kicked her legs and groaned. "I've been talking to this girl in my class. I thought we were friends 'cause we sit together at lunch and she shared her applesauce with me yesterday, but I heard her talking to two other girls about having a sleepover on Saturday, and they didn't invite me and I don't know why."

"Maybe they just have a special group thing going on," Lily offered.

"But I'm part of the group now," Sam complained. "At least I thought I was. I want a sleepover!"

Lily thought for a moment. "We'll have our own sleepover. Why don't we ask Grace?"

Sam brightened. "I like Grace!" she said. "Do you think she'd come?"

"I don't see why not," Lily said. "Let's go ask Mom and Dad!"

The two girls jumped up and ran into the kitchen.

28

Just Girls

The next day after school, Grace's mom was helping her pack her stuff for a sleepover with Lily and Sam. "Don't forget your pajamas," she said.

Grace was a little nervous as she stuffed her pajamas into her bag - it would be her first sleepover. "Should I bring anything else?"

Her Mom reached over to give her a big hug. "You are a wonderful, fabulous and amazing girl!" her Mom said. "They're going to love you and you're going to love them back and you'll be best friends forever. Trust me on that!"

Grace looked up at her Mom, eyes wide, and nodded slowly. Her Mom grabbed the bag and stood up. "Let's go!"

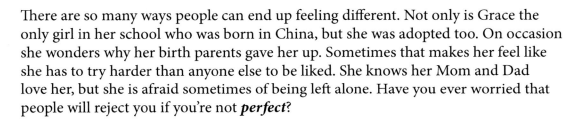

There are so many ways people can end up feeling different. Not only is Grace the only girl in her school who was born in China, but she was adopted too. On occasion she wonders why her birth parents gave her up. Sometimes that makes her feel like she has to try harder than anyone else to be liked. She knows her Mom and Dad love her, but she is afraid sometimes of being left alone. Have you ever worried that people will reject you if you're not *perfect*?

Try It On For Size

The doorbell rang. Grace and her Mom had arrived carrying a plate full of brownies and a suitcase packed with enough clothes for a week. As the girls stumbled up the stairs with Grace's things, it was hard to tell who had the biggest

smile. Once the brownies were gone, Lily pulled a big box out of the back of her closet.

"Yes!" Sam called out.

Grace tilted her head to the side. "What's that?" she asked.

Sam jumped in before Lily could reply. "That's Lily's costume collection! She has the coolest stuff!"

"And I got a few more things since we played last time. You wanna try some things on?"

"Yeah!" Grace and Sam said in unison.

29

Grace tried on a flowing, long powder-blue dress with sparkles. "This is so glamorous. Just like Carly Myers."

"Oh, I loved her in *Stars of Heaven*!" Lilly exclaimed. "Did you see it? She just won the *Teen Choice Award*."

Grace turned left and right in front of Lily's mirror. "I wish I could be an actress like her when I grow up."

"You can!" Sam encouraged Grace.

"Not really," Grace said. "Sometimes my Dad gets upset when there aren't many people who look like me on TV."

Sam danced and made funny sounds. "Why is that bad?"

Grace puckered her mouth. "I don't really want to talk about it."

"There aren't a lot of kids who look like us," said Lily.

"Well...I don't look like my parents," Grace said confidently. "But that's okay."

"What do you mean?" Sam asked.

"Well, I'm adopted."

Sam looked a little confused. "Oh that's cool."

Lily jumped in, "She didn't mean it like that. I don't think she noticed. We're mixed - half like you!"

Grace looked confused. "Oh, hmmm...come to think of it, I didn't notice that either!"

Sam jumped up and pulled her checkered skirt to her knees so she wouldn't trip over it as she walked over to the mirror. "I think we should make our own TV show."

"I think so too!" Grace said.

"That's a great idea!" Lily said. "Get into character; I'll do the filming on my phone."

They all struck a pose in the mirror before spreading around the room getting ready to make their first show.

After a lot of laughing and dancing, they finally fell asleep in Sam's room.

Everyone has dreams about what they want to do in their lives, whether it's for work or for a hobby. And those dreams change often, for most people. Just like you in many ways. You're always changing and growing. But sometimes it's hard to imagine those dreams if you never see anyone like yourself who's able to fulfill them. The girls were struggling with not feeling like there were any actresses like themselves who got leading roles. Do you have any dreams that are hard to imagine because you've never seen someone like yourself realizing them?

Brain Pickings

- What do you look for when you're making friends?
- Do you have friends that don't look like you?
- Is it easier to make friends with other kids who share your mixed race or mixed cultures?
- If you could be a celebrity, who would that be? Why?

Chapter 5: Emotion in Motion

Confusion is a complicated feeling. When I feel confused, my colors go all wonky, and it's pretty easy for others to notice. Humans show confusion in many different ways. Sometimes you can be angry or upset about something; but if you hold it in, you might end up thinking you're mad or upset about everything all at once. Sometimes you get butterflies in your stomach and your legs go all curly and if you try to sit still, you get all flushed. Some people may start to cry, some might get giddy. Those feelings of confusion can be pretty overwhelming, and often it's hard to talk about or express them to others. Your parents or friends might have to interpret what you're going through - figure out what your curly-legged, butterfly-stomach, laughing-crying, bug-eyed actions are all about. Talk about drama! Have you ever felt so confused?

Feelings & Confusion

Ethan's Mom recieved a phone call from school. She had to leave work and pick him up from the nurse's office. When they got home, she sat on the sofa looking at Ethan, who looked like he was working very hard not to cry.

"Honey," she sighed, "can you tell me what's going on?"

Ethan pressed his lips together, shook his head, stood up and started pacing. His mother was concerned. This was not the first time she'd seen him like this.

"Please sit," she said firmly. He relaxed his shoulders and sat.

"Was it something someone said?"

"This kid at lunch - he's always calling me names."

They stared at each other in silence for a few minutes until Ethan's Mom's cell phone began to ring. She glanced over and let it go to voicemail.

"Is that Dan?" Ethan asked sarcastically.

"Yes, honey."

"When do I get to see Dad again? I don't want Dan, I want Dad."

"There are some things you're not going to understand until you're older."

"I don't have any pictures to bring in for that stupid project for Miss Miller."

Ethan's Mom realized there might be something more going on than it seemed. "What project is that, honey?"

"Miss Miller wants us all to bring in pictures of us with our fathers and mothers to put up around the classroom to talk about our family trees." Finally Ethan couldn't hold it in any more and he started crying. "The other kids are really excited. They're talking about what their parents are like and what they do together. And then this girl told me that I used the wrong color pencil to draw Dad."

His Mom rushed over to him and held him in her arms, rocking him. "Oh, sweetie, I'm so sorry. I wish there were something - anything - I could do to make you feel better."

"I just want to be like everyone else."

Ethan's Mom continued rocking him and resolved to call the school the next day, to see if there was something the school could do about making this activity best for every type of family situation.

TALKING IT OUT; WORKING IT OUT

Let's see how our friend Luis helps Ethan deal with these feelings of confusion.

Luis picked up Ethan on the way to school the next morning. They were quiet for a while as they walked. Ethan was thinking about what his Mom said the evening before. "I think I made my Mom upset."

Luis looked at Ethan. "Parents are pretty understanding. What happened?"

Ethan stuffed his hands in his pockets. "I don't know."

Luis looked at him sideways. "You wanna tell me what you're really feeling? Sometimes that helps."

Ethan told him about the assignment with the pictures and how angry he was about having to explain being biracial to everyone. "Why should I have to choose anyway?"

Luis nodded. "Most people feel like they want to know everything. It's like, if they don't know they automatically get scared or something, and then they get all weird."

Ethan kicked a stone that was in his path and watched it skitter away. "It just makes me mad."

"I hear you," Luis said. "Wish I could do something."

Ethan was quiet.

"I'm mixed too, you know."

Ethan looked surprised. "Really?"

"Yeah, and it's confusing sometimes having to explain it to people. But I think most people are just curious."

"Maybe it's like not knowing why someone would like sports and theater," Ethan said.

"Yeah, like me!"

Ethan rubbed his face. "You think my Mom is mad at me?"

"Nah. She probably wants to make it easier for you."

Sharing The Mix

Sometimes you're in a situation that is really frustrating or that makes you angry, but there's nothing you can do to change it right away, especially if you don't know what caused it. When you feel this confused, talking with friends and family is good, but sometimes a physical activity can help you work out some of your stress. What do you do to help yourself feel better when you're confused, upset or even angry? Do you have a friend whom you can relate to, who shares similar experiences of feeling confused about how to explain being mixed to other people?

We've been learning some stuff in history class about slavery and colonialism. It's confusing because my father wants me to be proud of being African-American, and my mother wants me to celebrate British culture.
Malcolm in Chicago, Illinois.

Brain Pickings

- Have you ever had a time when a school activity made you feel different in a bad way?
- Do you ever find it difficult to deal with emotions sometimes, especially when you don't know what might make you feel a certain way?
- Adults have feelings too. Can it help to understand why your parents might be having difficult emotions?
- Does being mixed sometimes make you have conflicting emotions? Why is that?

Chapter 6: Strength In Numbers

Being mixed-race is not rare. There are millions of biracial and multiracial people in the United States, and many millions more around the world. In fact, two of the fastest growing groups in the United States are multiracial and multicultural households. And yet being mixed is not celebrated as much as being one race. For example, Black History Month is a very important way to remember and honor African-Americans who have made and still do make this country great. But what if you're African-American and something else? Having a group that you can identify with might make things a little easier for you in school and in your community. But you just may have to take the **initiative** to create this group. And in order to do that you'll have to find a **mentor** - an adult who can help you organize this group.

Mixed Challenge

Let's see how Luis, after speaking with Ethan, takes on this awesome challenge.

Luis jumped out of his chair the second the bell rang, and walked quickly to Ms. Mondet's office. She was the school counselor, and he thought she might have some good ideas about how to deal with Ethan's concerns.

"Hello Ms. Mondet!"

"Hi Luis! Excited as always!"

"So the other day Ethan was doing this project in school. Everyone was supposed to bring in a picture of themselves with their parents, but his Dad left them, like, a long time ago."

Miss Mondet nodded quietly.

"Then there's the biracial thing."

"What's the biracial thing?"

"Well, there are these guys in his class who are always bugging him to pick one or the other. He's both, you know. His Dad was Black, but he's not there, and his Mom is White and he's kind of, I don't know, maybe like me."

"What do you mean?"

"You know when you're two things...mixed," Luis continued.

"How do you feel about that?"

"Well, kind of good and kind of bad."

"You have mixed feelings about it?" Miss Mondet offered.

"I guess. It's just these guys have been hassling him about it."

"That sounds really frustrating. I wish he'd told me," Miss Mondet commented.

"I don't know. I think that might make it worse," Luis confessed.

"Why is that?"

"Because. There aren't too many kids like us around school."

"I think there are a lot more than you think. Everyone's just trying to do their best to blend in."

Luis shrugged. "Maybe."

"For example," Miss Mondet continued. "Did you know I'm half Japanese? But my father's Creole."

Luis looked surprised and didn't know what to say.

"I wanted to start a club for kids like you and Ethan, who have mixed ethnic and national backgrounds. What do you think?"

"A club? Like how?" Luis was intrigued.

"Just a place where kids could get to know each other. 'Cause you're really not alone, but I know you feel like you are. Then you guys can help each other come up with answers to these problems. I'm calling it the *Mixed Student Club.*

"Might work," Luis said noncommittally.

"I'd need to have an older kid to help me out, leading the group and getting other kids to join. It would be a lot of responsibility, though. Think you could help me with it?"

Luis thought he might be able to at least get Ethan to join. Maybe together they could find a couple of other people. "Like a mentor? Sure! I'll give it a try."

"Great! I'm happy about that. I'm glad we had the chance to talk." Miss Mondet filled out a hall pass for Luis and he headed back to his classroom.

Sometimes it's easier to see a problem than it is to know how to fix it. Getting people to work on a problem together can help get more ideas flowing and also make sure that no one thinks they are alone. Have you had any times when a group of people helped you solve a big problem? Have you ever started a group of your own? And I'm not talking about an ***Only Boys Who Like Smelly Cheese Sandwiches Club***, or in my case, ***Chameleons With A Weird Fashion Sense Only Club.*** When you share something you're passionate about, you can help change the world!

Being mixed can mean different things to different people. It's not necessary to explain it all to everybody, or even explain it at all. It's just important to be honest and happy with your mix. How people see you is not something you can fix - all you can do is help them understand. Just sharing your feelings can be like a huge weight taken off your shoulders. Which would not work for me because I don't have shoulders.

MIXING IT UP

After his meeting with Miss Mondet, Luis started thinking more about what it meant to be mixed. He remembered his Madre said there was a difference between looking mixed and feeling mixed. People might look at you and think you have all of this diverse background, but maybe you really feel like you're only one thing. But maybe you feel like you're connected to more than one background. He realized that he didn't just look mixed, he felt mixed too. He enjoyed doing things that came from both his Mom's and his Dad's side of the family. He liked Cuban food, like ropa vieja, and he liked Southern soul food, like fried okra. He also liked speaking more than one language. He needed to help Ethan and others to see that being mixed was a strength.

Luis told Ethan about Ms. Mondet's club, and then told Lily. Lily told Sam and Sam told Grace.

Then Grace told Oliver, which was a surprise to him. How did Grace know he was mixed? Or maybe she didn't. Either way, for the first time, Oliver felt like he really wanted to share his story with a classmate.

So, as they sat outside the library, Oliver with his dog Peanut, and Grace with her dog Scruffy, they traded stories. Grace's blended family came about through adoption. So she wasn't sure if she fit in because of that. She didn't know if being adopted *counted* as being mixed. And Oliver talked about being part Hopi. He held it in for so long, and now he was sharing his pride with someone who had a very different experience.

I belong to different packs. I have Black friends and Asian friends and white friends. They don't usually hang out together, but I can hang out with them. Sometimes it feels strange, but it can be fun fitting in.
Farzana in Portland, Oregon

BRAIN PICKINGS

- Have you ever sort of felt like you might belong to a particular group of people, but you weren't sure if you *counted* or fit?
- What's the first thing you share about yourself with another person when you know they're mixed too?
- Do you sometimes emphasize one aspect of your racial mix to some people and not to others? Why do you think that is?
- What can you learn about being mixed from your mentors and elders?

Chapter 7: Blending The Rules

When forming or joining a new group, everyone makes adjustments. Fitting in isn't just about your interests - it's about how you manage accepting new ideas, changing things that are familiar and of course meeting new people. For example, you might think it's easy for me to join a new crowd...but in fact, often it's easier to take my time getting to know everyone by listening in - and that's where my color-changing superpowers come in handy. Blending in can be tricky, but also fun. Multiracial and multicultural people can often blend into many groups because they feel like they are more than one.

IN THE MIX

Luis whistled as he put the rest of the snacks out. A big sign behind him read, *Mixed Student Club*. At 3:05, Luis saw Lily walking down the hall with another girl skipping in beside her. He suddenly felt self-conscious about being excited to see Lily. His voice quivered, "Hi, Lily!"

"Hi, Luis!" She then pointed at the skipping girl who had walked straight over to the snacks and opened a small bag of chips. "That's my sister, Sam. Sam, this is Luis."

"Hi, Luis," Sam said while crunching on a mouthful of chips. Then Grace walked in.

"Grace!" Sam ran over and pulled her toward the snacks.

Grace looked over at Lily and Luis. "Hey guys."

Ethan sauntered in next with Oliver, and they were followed by two other boys and a girl.

Grace walked over to the girl and hugged her. "Hi, Marianna. Have you met Lily?"

"I saw you out at recess a few times."

"Hey," Lily said.

Grace continued the introduction. "Marianna's folks come from Finland and she only moved here a year ago."

"Grace helps me to know what to do here. So much is different." Lily noticed that Marianna had an accent she'd never heard before. "You can call me Mari."

Luis grabbed Ethan and walked over to the other boys. "How's it going? I'm Luis and this is Ethan."

"Hi, I'm Tarek," said the shorter of the two.

"I'm Levi," said the tall, skinny kid.

"Thanks for coming!" Luis said. "What's your mix?"

Tarek laughed. "My Mom's Egyptian and my Dad's American."

Levi looked around the room. "I'm Jewish-Ethiopian."

"I'm Jewish too!" said Ethan.

Levi smiled. "Cool!"

Miss Mondet walked in just then, looking thrilled with the turnout. "Welcome everyone! Thanks for coming."

WORDS, WORDS, WORDS

"Don't forget the snacks!" she said. All the kids clamored to the snack table and grabbed handfuls of treats. Once they settled back into their seats, she smiled and sat on the edge of the table. "Thanks for setting everything up, Luis. Why don't we get started? Everyone pull up a chair."

There was a lot of shuffling around as the kids arranged themselves in a semi-circle around the room, facing Miss Mondet.

Miss Mondet was thrilled to know that the kids were eager to introduce themselves. She believed this was because

this group empowered them - gave them inner strength to be themselves. "Would anybody like to introduce themselves? Don't forget to mention how you identify yourself."

Tarek raised his hand "Hi! I'm Tarek. My mother is from Egypt, and my father is White American. I was born in Cairo, that's the capitol of Egypt, and came here when I was five. When I tell people I'm Egyptian, sometimes they say things that make me upset. I don't think they're trying to be mean, just funny, even though it's not funny at all. They think I ride camels, live in a pyramid and call my Mom 'Mummy.' Truth is I like XBox, football, hotdogs and hip-hop."

"Thank you, Tarek," said Miss Mondet. "That was a good example. Does anyone else have a story that can help explain how we sometimes feel mixed about sharing who we are and where we're from?"

Everyone's hands shot up. After they all introduced themselves, Miss Mondet stood up. "You've probably heard people use a lot of different words to describe the many ways in which people are mixed, but a lot of people don't realize they're mixing up the meanings of different words. For example, someone might ask what country you're from, when they really want to know why you look the way you do." She picked up a bag and started handing out slips of paper to all of the kids. When

she'd finished, she put some larger labels up on the blackboard. The labels were Nationality, Ethnicity, Culture, Race.

"Each of you has a few pieces of paper with words on it - in no particular order. What I'd like you to do is to organize them in the best way you can next to each of the labels up on the blackboard. Let's get started."

The kids looked at their sheets. Some giggled, some looked confused, but Luis jumped ahead. "Ok, seeing as I'm the leader..." Luis took his four sheets and ran up to the blackboard on which the four labels were taped. He taped *Asian* under *Race*; *Shoes off in house* under *Ethnicity*; *Great-Grandparents* under *Culture*, and *Korean* under *Nationality*.

Miss Mondet cocked her head to the side, "Almost, Luis. Think carefully."

Meanwhile, Lily arranged her sheets in order to match the labels, left to right. She walked up just as Oliver and Tarek arrived. They both struggled a bit with a couple of words - for Lily, it was Culture. She didn't know if eating pasta was part of Nationality or Culture. "Isn't pasta Italian?" She asked no one in particular.

Tarek replied, "I don't like pasta. I like flat bread. I think that's Culture."

"Pasta was invented in China," Miss Mondet suggested. "And Americans eat a lot of pasta."

Just behind them followed Mari, Ethan and Levi. Ethan first taped "French" under Culture. Then he looked around and got upset with a couple of the kids who snickered. "Hey, it's called French fries for a reason!"

Mari said, "We went to France for a vacation once, and I learned it's called Pommes Frites."

Levi asked, "Is Jewish a race? Like, it's not color, right?"

"I'm Black and Jewish!" said Ethan.

"So then what is it?"

"It's a religion. I have this sheet that says Jewish. So I think it should go..."

"Under Race!" said Sam.

Lily put her hand on Sam's shoulder, "You're not listening, Sis. It's, uh...I don't know..."

Miss Mondet smiled. "Culture is what you practice doing every day. And you might change in many ways throughout your life, including your culture."

"It's Culture!" Sam squealed while she jumped up and down.

"Very good!" Miss Mondet sat on the table next to the blackboard. "Multiracial is how you look and multicultural is how you act. So you see, labels are not easy. And in fact, they're just words. Labels don't tell your story. And I'm sure you all have really good stories! At our next meeting we're going to do an activity for which we don't use labels to learn about each other."

The kids didn't even realize their time was up as they excitedly continued trying to finish sorting their labels.

Most of us don't really think about the words we use to describe people. These words get used in a mishmash kind of way. Someone can have been born and raised in Sweden, but have family from any other part of the world.

Brain Pickings

- How would you categorize words like Latino, Australian, Catholic and Black? What about Russian, Brazilian, Filipino or Buddhist?
- What do you find exciting about getting others together who are mixed like you?
- In what ways do you change the words you use to describe yourself to different groups?
- When you see people on TV or videos who look mixed, do you try to identify *what* they are? If so, why? If not, why not?

Chapter 8: What Are We Anyway?

By early spring, Miss Mondet's *Mixed Student Club* had grown to fifteen kids. They had learned a lot about each other, and sometimes didn't even realize that other people could not really understand why the club was so good for them.

The kids sat in a big circle. Lily tried not to show her feelings about sitting next to Luis. She didn't want him to know that she liked him. Funny thing was that Luis was feeling the same way about her.

Miss Mondet introduced the topic of the meeting. "Does anyone remember the difference between *multiracial* and *multicultural*?"

Lily raised her hand. "Multiracial is how you look and multicultural is how you act."

Miss Mondet nodded her head. "Okay. So, being mixed can mean many things. Not just that your parents look different from each other, like, let's say, Asian and African-American, but also the things you like and do."

Ethan added, "My Mom likes to teach me how to say words in Yiddish. Like *mazel tov* is Yiddish for *congratulations*! That's cultural I think. But I'm also Black."

Luis chimed in, "My Dad says to say African-American… ."

Miss Mondet looked around the room, "What does everyone else think?"

A girl named Rayowa raised her hand, "I think being African is culture, like which country you're from. My mother is African - she's from Nigeria, but my father is African-American, from Atlanta, Georgia. They do things really differently. Sometimes they even fight about it. But then one of them usually stops and says 'Whoops! It's a cultural thing!' Then they talk about it. I think the race is Black."

Sam suddenly stood up. "There's this boy who told me that I'm not really Asian, and that I shouldn't be reading Japanese manga because I'm not from there and my Dad's Irish. But that boy's never been to Korea or Japan either. And he didn't even know The Philippines is near Japan, you know - in Asia. So, am I Asian because my Mom is Asian, or because I look a little Asian or because I like to read manga?"

Grace looked at Sam. "At least you look like you're a little of one thing and a little of another. Last year, my teacher called me up in front of the whole class to talk about Chinese New Year, but I don't know anything about it."

All of the kids in the room cringed and shook their heads.

"It's kind of silly, isn't it!" said Miss Mondet. "People sometimes assume you're supposed to act like you look."

Grace continued. "Well, there was this one time that was kind of funny. I was in this grocery store with my Mom. She was behind me looking at some magazines. There was this other woman, I think she was Chinese, in front of me digging in her purse for her credit card.

The woman at the cash register asked me if I liked helping my Mom shop. I said yes, and then she pointed to some strange-looking leafy thing the bagger was packing and asked me what it's called in Chinese. I said I didn't know, because my Mom doesn't speak Chinese, and neither do I. By then the woman in front of us had finished paying for her groceries and walked away.

The cashier told me I'd better go catch up to her. That's when my real Mom told me to move the cart up so she could finish putting our stuff on the counter. The cashier looked so embarrassed, but she didn't say anything. I told my Mom what happened later and we laughed our heads off."

Miss Mondet chimed in, "I don't think she was trying to be mean. She just wasn't expecting to see a mixed family. I think if the woman in front of you wasn't Chinese, she wouldn't even have noticed."

Luis entered the conversation. "There was a form my Mom had to fill out for me at the doctor's office. It had all these questions about race, and it was confusing. My Mom got frustrated and checked this category called Other. What is Other!?"

Tarek turned to Luis. "I think I'd have to pick Other too. I look pretty White, but I'm Egyptian."

Luis smiled, held up his hand and gave Tarek a high five.

My sister looks more Asian, and I look more Black. People often don't think we're sisters. Sometimes that makes me angry, and sometimes it makes me laugh.
Simone, in Boston, Massachusetts

BLENDED STORIES

It's nice when there's a group of people you can talk to about the things that bother or confuse you. Stories help people connect, even when your stories are different from those of your friends. Sharing your story with others who are like you can help you get over your mixed feelings about being...mixed! Now, my problem is that when I start talking, I just keep going. Like if I started telling you about where my parents, grandparents, great-grandparents are from, and where my 134 brothers, sisters and cousins live...take cousin Chilly - she's 9, she's an East Usambara Two-horned Chameleon and can change colors in like twice my speed, and my brother Charming has 58 children and I have to buy birthday presents twice a week! I have family that's Flapneck Chameleon, Meller's Chameleon, Panther Chameleon, Pygmy Chameleon, Veiled Chameleon... and then there's...OH LOOK! A DRAGONFLY!

BRAIN PICKINGS

- Can you share some stories about how strangers perceive you?
- What do you feel when someone assumes you're something you're not?
- Do you ever get defensive about an aspect of your identity when someone says something insensitive?
- How can you help others learn more about your mix?

Chapter 9: Wrapping It Up

I love hanging out in trees and listening to people tell stories. You and I also have stories and that's how we share our experiences with the world. We tell stories from our perspective of our experiences, and they often change. It could be like, "Drama drama drama!" Or like, "Ugh - draaaamaaaa." Or even like, "Like OMG, is that like DRAAMAA!" Being mixed gives us the opportunity to tell stories - stories that reflect our perspectives on interesting and colorful experiences we've had. We can share so many stories about ourselves and our families and friends!

Well, a year has gone by and it's the last day of school in Fairview. Can you believe it? I'm tearing up! All my new friends are going to be all over the place - going to camp, family trips, astronauting...Wait, seriously, if I were to go to Mars for summer vacation, I would just be bright red for, like, *months*. I like the diversity of colors on planet earth. Phew! Besides, I don't think I would like freeze-dried, squeeze-packaged astronaut space food.

51

MISS YOU ALREADY!

It was the last day of school. Sam couldn't believe the year had gone by so quickly. She sat on the front lawn, waiting for Lily. She was fidgeting nervously. Ethan came out of the school building and walked over to Sam. "Hi there! Looking forward to summer?"

"Yeah. I guess."

"You guess? It's gonna be great!"

"I don't know. We're going on a trip to um...Ireland."

"Oh cool. I'm going to camp," Ethan said. "There's all different stuff to do. I like canoeing and archery. But there's drama and science too."

Lily arrived and sat down next to Sam. "Hey, Ethan."

Ethan turned to Lily. "Sam said you're going away this summer. Where are you going?"

Lily shrugged. "My Dad's taking us to Ireland to meet some of our family over there."

Luis came up behind Lily and put his hand on her shoulder. Lily blushed.

"My Dad's taking us to meet some family in Ireland."

"Wow, where in Ireland?"

"Wexford."

Luis raised his eyebrows. "Hm. Can I go?"

Lily giggle. "Sure! I'll put you in Mom's suitcase!"

Ethan pointed at Luis. "Nah, he's going to Cuba. I'm so jealous!"

"I have family there," Luis said.

"My Mom's really excited." Luis looked at Lily again. "We should trade postcards. Like write down a little bit each day and send them to each other." Lily smiled broadly. "I'd like that!"

Ethan nudged Luis in the arm. "Hey, do I get to read them after?"

Sam looked back and forth between Luis and Lily. "Uuuuuuuuu!"

Just then Oliver and Grace walked up to the others. They were each carrying a piece of paper and comparing notes. Lily asked, "What are you guys looking at?"

Grace smiled and jumped up and down. "Miss Mondet helped Oliver and me get a volunteer job at the animal shelter for the summer!"

"Cool!" Sam said. "What's that?"

Oliver looked up from his paper. "I get to help with the dogs when they're going out in the yard to play."

"I get to help the groomers," Grace said.

Lily cut in. "I heard there's this bird reserve in Wexford, Ireland, where I'm going. I can take some pictures for you guys, if you want."

"That'd be great," Oliver said. "I wonder if they have the same birds there as they do here?"

"I think there's a lot of wet land there. So, maybe I'll see water birds," Lily added.

"Or mud birds," Luis cut in. "Is there such a thing as a mud bird?"

Lily laughed and punched him lightly on the shoulder.

"I guess we'll all be pretty busy this summer," Sam said, sounding a little disappointed.

"We'll have plenty of time after vacation to get together," Ethan assured her. "And think of everything we'll have to talk about!"

Tarek jogged by toward his Mom's car. "Bye guys! Have a good summer!"

"Where are you going?"

"Oh, going to visit my grandparents in Cairo!"

"Egypt!" Sam jumped up and down. "See, I remembered!"

Lily stood up. "Well, let's get going, Sam. Mom's waiting for us."

"Okay," replied Sam. Then with a hint of mischievousness whispered in Lily's ear, "Aren't you going to say goodbye to Luis?"

Luis reached out to take Lily's hand and Lily was about to kiss his cheek, when Sam turned red, grabbed her sister, and tugged at her. "Bye Luis..."

As the sisters started to walk away, Luis stumbled on his words and mumbled, "Have a good summer..."

"Wait up!" Grace called and she joined Sam and Lily. Then she turned and shouted, "See you soon, Oliver!"

As Grace put her arm around Lily's shoulder, Lily thought about how she'd made such good friends during their first year in Fairview. She couldn't wait to keep getting to know them better.

Pure You

Being mixed is not the most important point, but just being *YOU*, is. Nothing can change the real you - your dreams, desires and family. Just knowing that being biracial, multiracial or multicultural is common makes it exciting and fun, and helps you make friends of all kinds. I'm constantly adapting to all kinds of situations...but I'm always me - the serious, focused, never distracted, very recognizable me. Uuuu! Cricket! *Thwip! Slurp!* Wait...wait...I forgot I don't like cricket. I have very mixed feelings about my snack, now...this is not good...*Uurp!* Ugh...I better go...

Brain Pickings

- Are you nervous about making new friends? Why do you think that is?
- Do you rely on family to help you through these times when you get wrapped up in your emotions?
- What can you do to learn about your heritage or your parents' heritage over summer break?
- When watching TV, movies or videos, have you noticed an increase or not in the number of mixed people represented?

Being mixed is not about choosing this OR that.
Being mixed is about embracing this AND that!

Chapter 10: Words To Live By

Nationality: Samantha and Lily were both born in The Philippines, so they were Filipino citizens, but naturalized as US citizens. They are often asked about their nationality, as they spend half the summer in The Philippines, visiting family. But they don't know a lot about their mother's country, having come to the US when they were 3 and 6 years old. Nationality is not culture or race - what you look like does not determine how you live your life.

Religion: During the summer break, Ethan goes to synagogue every Saturday with Mom, and is already preparing for his Bar Mitzvah, but he doesn't look like most of the people who attend Torah services and Hebrew School. Race is not religion, as religion is not determined by what you look like.

Culture: Culture is how you live your life. Stories, especially movies and books, while they can be fun, do not change a person's culture, but can misrepresent them. For example, your culture or cultures are about not just *what* you eat, but about *how* you eat certain foods. Pasta meals are very common in Italian homes, but pasta was invented in China. At dinner in China, families that eat pasta dishes speak in Chinese, use chopsticks and interact differently, let's say, from a family having dinner in Italy where they speak Italian and eat with forks and knives. Language, religion, dance, music, clothes, weddings, school, family sizes and work, among many things, are different and similiar between cultures, in some ways.

Race: Luis' Mom has lighter skin and his Dad has darker skin, and Luis and his siblings are somewhere in-between. Race is usually determined by what you look like - skin color, shape of eyes, shape of the nose and texture of hair. The truth is that there's really only one race - the Human race, as Black people can be any shade, as can be Asians or Whites. Mixed-race kids can be any shade in between. For example, President Obama is Black and White - he's a biracial president.

Adoption: Grace is often asked about China, and is singled out as being *from* China. She's asked by some of the kids, as well as one of her teachers, if she went *home* during vacation (meaning China). Also, some of the kids talk about Harry Potter, and how his uncle and aunt were so mean to him, and if only his *real* parents had raised him, it would have been so much better. This makes Grace very upset because her parents have been absolutely amazing and supportive, and love her dearly.

Key Words

These words and more, and how they pertain to the mixed-race /mixed-culture experience, are explained on our Mixed Feelings website!
www.EntertainingDiversity.com/mixed-feelings.html

Adapting; Adaptation
African-American (Black)
Ambiguous
Archetypal; Archetype
Asian
Assets
Bias; Cross-Racial Bias, Cultural Biases
Biracial
Black (African-American)
Caucasian (White)
Code-Switch; Code
Compromise
Convert
Cross-Racial Adoption
Culture
Diversity
Empathy; Empathize
Empowering; Empowerment

Group Culture
Hispanic
Initiative
Interpret
Mentor
Mixed-Race
Mixed-Culture
Multiracial
Must-Do-Culture
Native American
Other
Perspective
Race, Races
Resilience
Stereotypical; Stereotype
TCK (Third Culture Kid)
Want-To-Do-Culture
White (Caucasian)

Enrich Your Mixed Family!

www.EntertainingDiversity.com/mixed-feelings.html

- Important keywords used in the book
- Discussion topics
- Activities for kids
- Activities for parents
- Educational materials for teachers
- Website links (extensive list of links)
- Guides & Resources
- Facebook engagement

About Teja Arboleda, MEd

Teja founded Entertaining Diversity, Inc., in 1993 to provide entertaining ways in which to explore and celebrate diversity. He is a television producer, professor, illustrator, nationally acclaimed keynote speaker and an expert on race culture. Teja has an Emmy Award and two Telly Awards for PBS educational programming. He is the author of *In The Shadow of Race* and *Jeni So Many*, both of which address multiracial and multicultural identity. Teja is African-American/Native-American and Filipino-Chinese and German-Danish, and he grew up in Japan. He lives in Massachusetts with his wife Barbara and their daughter Katie.

Teja Arboleda is available for:
- Speaking engagements
- Media interviews
- Consulting on site
- Consulting via Skype and Google Hangouts

Subject matters of interest for healthy mixed family building:
- Multiracial / Biracial parenting advice
- Multicultural family conflict resolution
- TCK (Third Culture Kid) support
- Cross-racial adoption parenting advice

For more information on Entertaining Diversity, please visit or contact:
www.**EntertainingDiversity**.com
e-mail: info@EntertainingDiversity.com

The author (on right) wearing diapers.

The author (on right) wearing a yukata in Japan.

The author (on right), post-Germany, wearing Lederhosen in NYC.

Other books by Teja Arboleda

Jeni So Many

For early learners.
Jeni is many. One day while on an adventure, she learns she can make new friends by finding similarities, while staying uniquely Jeni.

Jeni So Many is dedicated to the many millions of people around the world who consider themselves 'mixed'. Multiracial, multiethnic and multicultural families, adopted families and 'blended' individuals are the ambassadors of all people.
ISBN-13: 978-0692620274 (Entertaining Diversity, Inc.)
Purchase: www.createspace.com/5996469

In The Shadow Of Race…Again

For adults.
For once it's not just Black and White.
This is a follow-up to Arboleda's compelling chronicle of his journey through life as a multicultural American. Arboleda uniquely and personally challenges institutionalized notions of race, culture, ethnicity, and class. He fleshes out the depth of his experience as a culturally and racially mixed American, illustrating throughout the enigma of cultural and racial identity and the American identity crisis.

Parallel to some experiences of the first multiracial, multicultural and multiethnic US President, Barack Obama, Arboleda adds stories of America's struggle to tackle complex issues of race in the shadow of 9/11, *#Black Lives Matter*, *#OscarsSoWhite* in history, the N-word, freedom of speech and immigration.

Available in September, 2016.